Matthew 18

A Conversation Between a Survivor of Childhood Sexual Abuse and a Catholic Bishop

Carrie Bucalo and
Bishop Bill Muhm

Published by
Hybrid Global Publishing
333 E 14th Street
#3C
New York, NY 10003

Manufactured in the United States of America, or in the United Kingdom when distributed elsewhere.

Bucalo, Carrie.
Muhm, Bishop Bill.
Matthew 18
     ISBN: 978-1-957013-81-7
     eBook: 978-1-957013-82-4
     LCCN: 2023908201

Cover design by: Julia Kuris
Copyediting by: Claudia Volkman
Interior design by: Suba Murugan
Carrie Bucalo Author photo by: Jessica Rhine Photography
Photographer Credit for Interior Images: Jenifer Cady Photography
Bishop Bill Muhm Author photo by: Matthew Barrick

www.healedbytruth.com

*Dedicated to all survivors of sexual abuse
at the hands of those who represent the Church*

Endorsements

Matthew 18 is presented as "a face-to-face conversation between a survivor of sexual abuse at the hands of someone who represented the Church, and a Catholic bishop." If only this would happen more often throughout the Church, and around the world! Both Carrie and Bishop Muhm point out the importance of healing, trust, and the Passion of Jesus, which encompasses the pain of victims and survivors. In this conversation, Jesus Himself becomes *a source of new life.*

—Father Christopher L. Zugger, author of *Finding a Hidden Church* and *The Forgotten*

Matthew 18 is a courageous, honest, creative, and powerful exchange between an abuse survivor and a bishop in the Catholic Church. In the aftermath of COVID-19, when hidden traumas are surfacing daily, this conversation is a balm of hope. It is a dialogue "without masks" in which the reader is permitted to be like Thomas the Apostle and touch the wounds of the resurrected Jesus.

—Rita A. Simmonds, award-winning poet and author of *Convicted by Mercy*

A much-needed dialogue between clergy and survivors of sexual abuse in the Catholic Church. As a survivor myself, the trauma is so deep-seated that it is hard to process internally, much less share publicly. Carrie, in her brilliance, weaves her artwork into her story of courage as she allows her love of Jesus to triumph over the pain. A stunning piece of inspired words and visual artistry.

—Erin Merrill, blogger and founder of
CatholicHoneyBadger.com

It seems impossible to discover treasures when we talk about child abuse, especially child sexual abuse. But here, on the pages of *Matthew 18*, Carrie and Bishop Muhm uncover a path of healing and hope! There's so much to learn about childhood trauma, healing, and forgiveness. I personally believe there's no better place to start than with the Gospel message. Thank you both for sharing your words of healing.

—Dena Braeger, Major Retired, combat Veteran,
Protestant children's pastor, and mother of six

The beauty and reality of God's hand in this book utterly surprises me. I am happy to find joy and hope in these pages. I feel heard, and I have found hope for my children and for the Church. Thank you, Carrie and Bishop Muhm, for being a voice for everyone who has suffered.

—Mother of three young survivors of child sexual
abuse in the Catholic Church

This book will change and save lives and spirits! Carrie and Bishop Muhm create a place of acknowledgment and peace in an enormously difficult space. I'm grateful to

Carrie for sharing her story that will buoy many, including those like me whose close family members have been deeply wounded by clerical sex abuse but for whom leaving the Church is not an answer. Our Lord's words in Matthew 18, as seen through the lens of child abuse survivors, are brilliant! As they explain, Jesus foresaw and carried the pain of these survivors. I was particularly moved by the chapter on forgiveness. May the Lord continue to bless and inspire Carrie and Bishop Muhm in their amazing healing ministry!

—D.P., sister of an adult survivor of child sexual abuse by a Catholic priest

This book will change lives. It has changed mine. As a survivor of childhood sexual abuse at the hands of someone who represented God to me, I live with emotional, psychological, and spiritual wounds that affect my life every day. However, to quote chapter one, "What seems to have been a wreckage of my humanity, Christ has turned into an opportunity for hope."

The story of abuse does not end with pain. In *Matthew 18*, Carrie and Bishop Muhm do a fantastic job discussing how Christ meets and calls survivors, and those who desire to support them, into his light and truth. There is hope for beauty and healing amid this pain that would be unbearable apart from Christ. This book shows what that healing is meant to look like in Christ. God has used *Matthew 18* to show me parts of my wounded heart that need more of His light. I intend to keep this book nearby for years to come. I know more healing will come to me and others through its pages.

—R.W., adult survivor of child sexual abuse in the Catholic Church

Contents

Introduction

Bishop Bill Muhm

In 1989, I entered seminary in formation for priestly ministry in the Archdiocese of New York and the Archdiocese for the Military Services, USA. During my first year in the seminary, one of my classmates, (now Father) Richard Veras introduced me to a number of his friends who were faithful Catholic laypeople living and working in the New York metropolitan area. These friends were all, to some extent, involved in an international Catholic lay movement called Communion and Liberation (CL). One of these friends was a young woman named Rita Flansburg. Rita and I became friends. However, during my years as a Navy chaplain, I made little effort to stay connected with her or the other CL friends I had made in New York.

In 2011, Carrie Bucalo and her husband, Justin, and their young family became friends with Rita Flansburg, who was now known by her married name, Rita Simmonds. Carrie was introduced to Rita by Heather King as she was looking for other artists and writers who could help her with her new "Healed by Truth" ministry.

In 2019, after I retired from service as a chaplain in the Navy, I was called to be an auxiliary bishop for the Archdiocese for the Military Services, USA. I was assigned to shepherd the Catholic U.S. military communities in Europe and Asia. I was still learning my new territory and getting to know my new flock when I visited U.S. Army Garrison Bavaria in Hohenfels, Germany, for the first time in February 2020. After Sunday Mass, I met some of the faithful who had attended that day. Among them were Carrie Bucalo and her family. Carrie asked me, "Bishop, do you know Rita Simmonds?" That common friendship with Rita Simmonds was the start of my friendship with Carrie and Justin, a U.S. Army soldier, and their six children, two of whom I eventually confirmed in Hohenfels. The Lord certainly works in mysterious ways!

As we got to know each other, Carrie revealed to me that she had been sexually abused as a child by her father, who was a prominent member of his Catholic parish in Albuquerque, New Mexico, when Carrie was growing up. Although Carrie's father was not an ordained minister, he represented the Church in Carrie's eyes, because he was a leading lay minister in their parish. As would be expected, the abuse left deep scars on Carrie's heart and soul. Carrie shared with me that for her entire adult life she had struggled to come to terms with the abuse and to integrate the trauma into her Catholic faith life, which had remained strong throughout her childhood and adult life. I marveled at the resiliency of Carrie's faith and her willingness to share her personal history in a public way.

In late 2020, Carrie became very ill with COVID-19 and was hospitalized. During her recovery, she had time to meditate on Scripture. One particular chapter of the Gospel of Matthew had attracted her attention. She came to believe that this one chapter presented "in a nutshell" a comprehensive summary of Our Lord's teaching on the scourge of child sexual abuse that has afflicted the world and the Catholic Church for many years—but had come to widespread public awareness for the first time in the spring of 2002, following a prominent series of articles in the *Boston Globe*.[1]

Carrie was convinced that Our Lord foresaw the current crisis in the Church and that He spoke about it in this particular chapter of the Bible: Matthew 18. Although Carrie had not been abused by a priest, she had survived abuse by someone who represented God and the Church.

Carrie convinced me that Our Lord foresaw this current time of crisis in the Church and spoke to His disciples (past and present) about it in Matthew 18. She asked me to engage in an extended "conversation" with her about what the Lord might be telling today's

---

1 The crisis of 2002 resulted in the United States Conference of Catholic Bishops (USCCB) creating the "Dallas Charter," which was a commonly agreed-upon set of procedures for U.S. bishops to follow when allegations of child sexual abuse had been raised against a Catholic priest in the United States. The crisis of 2002 seemed to "die down" gradually until the summer of 2018, when allegations against former Cardinal Theodore McCarrick became publicly known, and the "Pennsylvania Grand Jury Report on Sexual Abuse of Children by Catholic Priests" was released. These events of 2018 made it clear that the crisis of 2002 involved more than alleged abuse by priests— the events of 2018 revealed that bishops had also apparently been personally guilty of abuse and also of neglecting to use proper pastoral oversight to ensure that priests who had abused children were removed from public ministry.

survivors who had suffered sexual abuse as children at the hands of people who represented the Church—and what Our Lord was telling the Church at large. What did these thirty-five verses of Matthew 18 have to say today to these survivors? How could a Catholic bishop, who represents the hierarchy of the Church, contribute to this conversation and to the healing of adult survivors?

Carrie and I agreed to present our conversation as just that—a face-to-face conversation between a survivor of sexual abuse at the hands of someone who represented the Church, and a Catholic bishop.

Our conversation is not primarily intended to prevent anyone from being abused in the present or future—although of course that is very important and what everyone should want and strive for. Rather, our conversation is an attempt to help today's adult survivors of sexual abuse at the hands of someone who represented the Church to become fully alive in Christ. In other words, our conversation is not rooted in a legal or psychological perspective; it is rooted in a Gospel perspective: What does Our Lord say in Matthew 18 to present-day survivors?

If our conversation is rooted in the Gospel, it makes sense to start with a more fundamental question: What exactly is the Gospel? What is Scripture, and where did it come from?

When I was growing up in Denver, Colorado, my dad would tell family and friends some very interesting and adventurous things that had happened to him when he was a boy and a young man. Dad was a good storyteller. He would tell his stories at family gatherings, on road trips, and around the campfire on weekend trips to the mountains. These stories were quite amazing, and they enthralled both children and adults.

When my dad was in his late seventies, he retired and had time on his hands. To his credit, he decided to write down these stories for my sisters, nieces and nephews, and me so the stories would not be lost when we couldn't remember them anymore. He spent hours typing them up, and he emailed them to us. When Dad passed away in 2009, my sister Kathy had a brilliant idea: Why not combine all the stories into a printed booklet and offer a copy as a gift to those who attended Dad's memorial service? That's exactly what we did. Everyone who received the booklets loved reading them, and to this day I treasure them in both printed and electronic formats.

The four books of the Gospels we have today (Matthew, Mark, Luke, and John) were written in the same way. As most people probably know, Our Lord Jesus Christ was born on earth more than two thousand years ago. He lived His life as a carpenter's son and as a carpenter in His own right. When He was about thirty years old, He began His public ministry. During these few brief years, He preached and taught, healed the sick, fed the hungry, cast out demons, raised the dead, and worked other miracles. Finally, He was crucified, died, resurrected, and ascended into heaven.

The disciples observed and remembered His words and actions while He lived here on earth. After His ascension into heaven, they passed down their memories of what He said and did to the younger generation in the form of "oral history," or stories told around the campfire. Later, they began to realize the need to write down these stories. If not, they would be lost with the passage of time. The four Gospels we have today were written, under the inspiration of the Holy Spirit, by those who had heard and remembered the stories told "around the campfire."

Our Church teaches that the four Gospels are products of selection, synthesis, explanation, and proclamation. However, as the word of God written under the inspiration of the Holy Spirit, they tell us the honest truth about the words and actions of Jesus. Moreover, there is infinite depth of meaning embedded in sacred Scripture, because all of Scripture is the inspired word of God. New meanings are "unpacked" by new generations of believers as the centuries unfold.

Both Carrie and I have come to believe that Our Lord really did have today's crisis in mind when he spoke the words of Matthew 18 almost two thousand years ago. We believe that those to whom Our Lord was speaking include twenty-first-century adult survivors of sexual abuse at the hands of those who represented the Church, as well as to the twenty-first-century Church at large. We believe that what Our Lord has to say is extremely important—that He wants each one of His lost sheep back and fully alive in Christ! We invite all survivors of sexual abuse at the hands of someone who represented the Church to join our conversation and consider whether Our Lord is speaking to them. Carrie and I believe that He is! We are certain that Our Lord wants each survivor back, fully alive in Him and His Church!

We also invite everyone, including those who were never abused by anyone, and non-Catholics, into our conversation. This present time of crisis and sadness is also a time of extraordinary grace for all of us: "Where sin abounds, grace abounds all the more" (Romans 5:20).

CHAPTER ONE

Jesus and the Child

At that time the disciples approached Jesus and said, "Who is the greatest in the kingdom of heaven?" He called a child over, placed it in their midst, and said, "Amen, I say to you, unless you turn and become like children, you will not enter the kingdom of heaven. Whoever humbles himself like this child is the greatest in the kingdom of heaven. And whoever receives one child such as this in my name receives me."

(Matthew 18:1–5)

Bishop Muhm: Carrie, it's good to speak with you in person without masks! After years of talking virtually and wearing masks, I'm glad to have the opportunity to engage in this important conversation face-to-face with you. After all, we are destined for eternal life without masks, when we see Him face-to-face in the Kingdom of Heaven (see Revelation 22:4).

It's tragic that children have been gravely harmed by ordained and lay ministers in the Catholic Church. This injustice cries out to heaven, and it breaks my heart. I, as a successor to the apostles, offer you and all victims of abuse my heartfelt apology. Children belong to Christ and to His Church. If there's any way the Church can succeed in inviting them back, we must move heaven and earth to do so.

In Matthew 18:1–5, Christ teaches us very clearly about the place of children in the Kingdom of Heaven. As much as the abuse of a child angers and distresses Our Lord, He is overjoyed when His children are loved, respected, healed, and cared for. We, the Church, must persevere in working to make this ideal a reality.

I'm sorry that you felt unaccompanied during the darkness of your childhood. Thank you for trusting Christ and His Church. Thank you also for trusting me. Although you were betrayed and abandoned by those who represented the Church, Christ never betrayed nor abandoned you; He will never betray nor abandon anyone. Just as you have relearned to trust, we all must relearn to trust. Why should we settle for a broken, wounded Church when Christ can heal us?

Carrie: Bishop Muhm, from the bottom of my heart, thank you. I cannot tell you how much healing and light your friendship brings me. Matthew 18:1–5 has been a difficult place for me to stand. In my childhood, I had a sense that Christ was different from what my abusers told me about Him, but the suffering and the pain of the abuse were often too much for me to bear. I felt like running away from Christ. I feared Him. I did not want Him to touch me.

It has taken His whole mystical body, the Church, to convince me that I should stay. My brothers and sisters in Christ have shown me God's face and ministered to me in ways they could never imagine. I'm especially struck by those who have refused to live their lives without Christ, even when they faced impossible circumstances. They gave a witness to loving and befriending Christ even if it seemed like their lives would be destroyed because of it, and each time, something remarkable happened.

I see these living witnesses all around me, in my everyday life. My "hundredfold" family has come through. Justin takes the time to help me on my bad days, even though he has his own crosses to carry. He patiently fills in the gaps, and I am speechless. I have countless friends who have gone out of their way to help me, especially when my spiritual and emotional wounds were debilitating. And even you, Bishop, bring me joy on some of my darkest days, and I cannot tell you how much good it does my soul.

I would be remiss if I did not tell you how much I love God, and how much Christ has healed me *within* His Church. What seems to have been a wreckage of my humanity, Christ has turned into an opportunity for hope. I am relearning to trust every day. I sense that, as broken as I am, I'm already sitting in Christ's presence in the Kingdom of Heaven. I trust that one day I will be fully healed and will see Him face-to-face in the Kingdom of Heaven with the peace and calm of the child in Matthew 18.

Bishop Muhm: Carrie, I'm amazed by your trust! Because I represent the Church, I know it takes a lot of faith for you to proceed with this conversation. I intend to honor your trust and hope to help the Lord in some small way in His work of making you whole.

The term *Kingdom of Heaven* has enormous meaning and value for all of us. It means the new creation, the right relationship between God and His people on earth. In other words, when human lives, human activity, and human society are properly aligned with God's will, then God's healing and redeeming grace will flow uninhibited through the world to set things right. When a broken, sinful world is brought into alignment with reality, then God will be able to work many miracles through His people, the Church. In this way, the ministry of the Church makes the Kingdom of Heaven present here on earth in a real but incomplete way.

The Kingdom of Heaven began on earth when God called Abraham to be the father of God's Chosen People, the Jews. It progressed as the Jewish people learned to put their faith in God and obey His will. It took a giant step forward when God became a man at Bethlehem. The Kingdom of Heaven reached its climactic moment in the death and resurrection of Jesus Christ two thousand years ago. It continues to unfold today in the world through the ministry of the Church whom Jesus Christ established upon His ascension to His Father's right hand, and through Pentecost. The Kingdom of Heaven will finally attain total fulfillment when Our Lord Jesus Christ comes in glory at the end of time to inaugurate absolute justice, absolute truth, and absolute goodness in a new heaven and a new earth.

So, even though the Kingdom of Heaven began thousands of years ago, we are still waiting for it to reach its fulfillment. In the meantime, maybe we could define the Kingdom of Heaven as the ongoing renewal and redemption of the human race—or as things gradually becoming the way they're supposed to be.

One of the signs of the Kingdom of Heaven is that people grow toward becoming the way God made them to be. One very important component of this transformation is the ability to trust. God designed the human person to trust. When we trust, we act in sync with our deepest human nature. This is easy to see in children. They are naturally "wired" to trust. They also express their emotions quite readily and unselfconsciously. When we observe them trusting others, we can see that they're happy and free. On the other hand, when we observe children being distrustful of others, we can see that they're unhappy.

Tragically, adults have betrayed the trust of children in many ways. Probably the worst possible betrayal by adults of childlike trust is sexual abuse. In recent times, society has come to realize that sexual abuse of children by adults has been pandemic throughout human history. One way in which victims are left broken by this outrage is that they lose their ability to trust. We cannot live without trust.

When I was a Navy Chaplain Candidate, I spent the summer of 1992 interning at a Naval Hospital. One of the chaplains showed a training video to sailors going through rehabilitation for alcohol dependency. The video, produced by the Church of Jesus Christ of Latter-day Saints, is titled *The Consequences of Our Choices* (or *The Pump*).[2] In this eight-minute video, a man dying of thirst faces a dilemma: either trust written instructions left by someone he doesn't know—and possibly live—or refuse to trust and certainly die. At the beginning, the video shows a message saying: "If you trust too much,

_____
2 https://www.youtube.com/watch?v=Xa8XiSKAR68.

too easily, you will live to be deceived. But if you do not trust enough, you may not live at all."

People who have trusted and then been victimized can lose their ability to trust. No one could blame them for doing so. But those who lose their ability to trust are missing out on the fullness of life. The wisdom of the world says that trust is immature and unrealistic—while refusal to trust is mature and realistic. But the exact opposite is true in the Kingdom of Heaven!

The Kingdom of Heaven—the new creation—is the real world. In the Kingdom of Heaven, children teach everyone to trust. Jesus illustrates this by teaching about the Kingdom of Heaven in the presence of a child. Everyone must unlearn the wisdom of the world—and learn (or relearn) that trust leads to happiness in the Kingdom of Heaven.

Guarded
Watercolor on cold press
by Carrie Bucalo

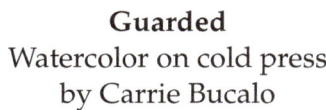

Carrie: I painted this piece to show how guarded my heart can be. I'm a pretty trusting person, and I think people consider me to be open and vulnerable. But deep down inside, I struggle to let anyone in. I've gone through too much pain, betrayal, and broken relationships to leave my heart out in the open. Sometimes my heart feels like a caged prison, drifting into outer space. As an abuse survivor, I deal with dissociation in my everyday life. Something or someone will frighten me, and I think, *I'm out of here!* My heart drifts away, detached from my body, in a cold and lifeless realm.

But I have hope! And even though I've been wounded in the worst ways, I still think I'm beautiful. The bright yellow sunflowers sprout from deep within my heart and reveal my true colors. There is still life inside of me! And if someone has the right key, maybe I'll open back up (as demonstrated by the heart-shaped keyholes in the center of the flowers). As cold and as lifeless as my heart might proclaim me to be, I'm dying inside to be found, to be looked at, to be understood, heard, appreciated, and loved. In a word, I'm dying to trust!

Even a heart like mine can learn to trust again. And some of the people in my life have found the right key. My husband's honesty and vulnerability in front of me have opened my heart to marriage, children, and family. My children's affection and helplessness in my arms opened my heart to the beauty of motherhood. My friends' determination and great love for me has opened my heart to the world.

I believe that every wounded heart needs the right key, and that's why I have hope for all survivors of abuse, for our Church, and for our world. The "keys to the Kingdom" are our ability to trust God and one another.

CHAPTER TWO

Sexual Abuse of a Child

"Whoever causes one of these little ones who believe in me to sin, it would be better for him to have a great millstone hung around his neck and to be drowned in the depths of the sea. Woe to the world because of things that cause sin! Such things must come, but woe to the one through whom they come! If your hand or foot causes you to sin, cut it off and throw it away. It is better for you to enter into life maimed or crippled than with two hands or two feet to be thrown into eternal fire. And if your eye causes you to sin, tear it out and throw it away. It is better for you to enter into life with one eye than with two eyes to be thrown into fiery Gehenna."

(Matthew 18:6–9)

Bishop Muhm: Carrie, it's good that we're having this conversation in person, which is very important both for victims of abuse and for the Church. In this conversation, you speak not only for yourself; you also speak on behalf of other victims of sexual abuse at the hands of Church ministers. Written and virtual communication is very important—especially in times of pandemic—but personal encounter can heal people in a way that long distance communication cannot.

Maybe you and other victims have felt alone, isolated from Christ and His Church. Maybe you felt that what happened to you in the past was overlooked or dismissed by the Church as of no importance. Maybe you felt that no one cared.

If so, I can certainly understand that. Although I was never sexually abused by anyone, in the past I have been on the receiving end of abusive behavior. I can understand victims feeling overlooked or abandoned.

I hope these verses from the Gospel of Matthew will offer hope to you and to other victims of sexual abuse at the hands of Church ministers. You are not alone. Christ had you and other victims, and His entire Church, in mind during His public ministry, His Cross, and His Resurrection.

Carrie: Bishop Muhm, I appreciate your words and your willingness to talk with me about these things, and I'm sorry to hear that you have suffered from abusive behavior. It hurts me to hear that. I can see that your sufferings have left a lasting mark, as well as an opening in your heart for others like me. In this place of woundedness, we have a space for this conversation. Thank you for accompanying me, and I hope I can accompany you as well.

The words of harm and abuse are very hard to take in. We have to be brave to speak and brave to listen.

The hardest thing to hear are the stories of children who were gravely harmed by the adults in their life who were supposed to care for them. They are shattered in ways no one can imagine. Their wounds weigh on their entire lives like the heavy millstone Jesus talks about in Matthew 18. This wound is crushing.

I'm thankful that Our Lord talked about child sexual abuse and became visibly present to all children who suffer in this way, and that the Gospel writer Matthew was able to capture His words in chapter 18. Sexual abuse is one of the most traumatizing things a human being can go through, especially for a "little one" who believes in God.

My father came from a troubled home. His father was unhappy, and I've been told that he hated all religion and forbade any talk of God in their home. My father struggled in school, in friendships, and in life. Early on, he turned to drugs, sex, and alcohol to try and solve his problems.

My mother grew up down the street from my father, in a loving Protestant home. From what I've gathered from family members, my father began sexually abusing my mom when she was around four years old. My dad was just a child himself and was likely sexually abused by someone in his family, or by someone the family trusted. As it so often happens, sexual abuse is something that can be handed down from one generation to the next. The abuse started in my parents' childhood and carried on into their adult years.

After my parents got married, they moved to Albuquerque, New Mexico, before I was born, drawn by the sunshine and the beautiful weather. They weren't expecting to find the Catholic faith, but they did. Catholic culture in New Mexico has deep roots, which are just as much a part of the land as they are a part of the people. Moved by the beauty and richness of the people's faith, my parents converted in the early 1980s.

My father seemed to have a deep spiritual charisma, and he immediately dove into the mysteries of the Catholic faith. He was moved by the local people's devotion to Our Lady. Unfortunately, the sexual violence of his childhood had warped his mind and heart, twisting his perception of right and wrong. He had never understood that sexual acts done to a child were wrong. Both of my parents seemed to believe that they could do whatever they wanted with their bodies and the bodies of their children, including their sexuality, without any consequence whatsoever. My father would even go so far as to tell me one day that his sexual acts done to me as a child were his—and God's—expression of "love."

The only reason I share this with you, Bishop, is so that you see how gravely twisted and damaged my father's sexuality and faith really were. People wonder how things like this can happen. This is how they happen.

This was the mess I was born into. My father began sexually abusing me in my earliest memories of childhood, most likely starting in my infancy. My mother knew no different and allowed him to do whatever he wanted. My father had a great web of lies, manipulations, and cultlike control over me and my sisters. My mother was neglectful and the perfect enabler. I was not allowed to ask questions, or "share our secret" with anyone. My father threatened me with my life if I ever spoke about the things he did to me. When I was a teenager, he told family members, friends, and people in the community the most awful lies about me so no one would trust me or believe me if I did speak.

People wonder how sexual predators keep their victims silent. This is how they keep them silent. It's not that hard to keep a child silent. A child cannot process trauma and abuse. A child doesn't have the proper tools to communicate it. And if they do speak, no one listens to them because of the lies their abuser tells about them. Who would believe a child over a trusted adult? This is really one of the most helpless and painful human experiences possible—to be a child who is abused and betrayed, who speaks but is punished and no one listens.

Before long, my father became an active lay minister at our local Catholic Church. He was an usher, lector, altar server, Bible study leader, RCIA sponsor, Marriage Enrichment leader—and because he physically looked like Jesus, with his long hair and beard, he played the role of Jesus in our parish Passion Plays.

Dear Bishop, I am sad to tell you that because my father was a minister in the Catholic Church, because he resembled Jesus as a man, and because he wove in the abuse with the mysteries of our Catholic faith, his abuses gravely harmed my mind, body, and soul. My father wounded me in the depths of my being. It changed the way I saw myself, my family, my community, God, and the Catholic Church.

Years of abuse changed the way I could feel loved by God and the Church. The sacred mysteries of our faith became torturous. Why did my father have to twist my Catholic faith to abuse me? Why did he look like Jesus? To be wounded with an image of God who is wounded is beyond anything I can describe. In a spiritual sense, my eyes, my hands, my feet, my whole being were thrown into the flames of a hellish fire because of the things my father did (see Matthew 18:8–9). Everything about God and about my faith was stripped of its comfort and beauty.

People wonder how it's possible for ministers in the Church to abuse children. This is how it's possible. We all know from the past two decades that certain bishops, priests, deacons, religious, and lay ministers like my father have done terrible things to children. Like my father, these individuals have desecrated the face of the Father, they have desecrated Christ's face on the Cross, they have desecrated the beauty of the Spirit, and they have desecrated the innocence and trust of helpless children.

It would seem, Bishop, that "the Cross has been emptied of its power," that the Church has been defeated. The father of lies seems to have had the upper hand. And yet, this is *not* the end of my story. I am here to tell you that this does *not* have to be the end of any survivor's story. On the contrary, because the Cross of Christ was not emptied of its power, this is the story of how we can get everything back, and I mean ALL of it. I can't wait to tell you more!

Bishop Muhm: Carrie, I am very sorry that the sexual abuse you suffered as a child has wounded you so deeply. At the same time, I'm encouraged by your unshakable lifetime commitment to your Catholic faith.

I am also encouraged that Matthew 18:6–9 seem to suggest that Jesus had you individually—and all victims of sexual abuse at the hands of Church ministers, both individually and collectively—in mind during His earthly life, death, and Resurrection.

In verses 6–9, we see two ideas recorded consecutively: the seriousness of leading a child into sin, and the seriousness in general of sins of impurity. Both ideas are presented using extreme images.

In verse 6, the image of the millstone is extreme. A millstone was very large and heavy; anyone tied to one and cast into the sea would have no hope of survival. In other words, Our Lord seems to say that an adult who intentionally leads a child into sin is himself in a hopeless moral predicament, with no chance of survival. The theological term for such a moral predicament is mortal sin.

Some victims or survivors might mistakenly think that Our Lord is referring to them in verses 6–7, that they are somehow to blame for the abuse. Some may have even heard this from their abusers. But we can be absolutely sure that Our Lord is NOT saying this; in these verses Our Lord is referring to the abuser—not to the victim or survivor.

Verses 6–9 use extreme images. Cutting off a body part or gouging out an eye would cause irreversible damage to a person. The idea of intentionally cutting off one's hand or foot, or gouging out one's eye, is unthinkable. No one in their right mind would entertain such thoughts, nor would the Lord want anyone to. Instead, these verses seem to condemn sins of sexual impurity in the strongest possible terms. Cutting off one's hand likely refers to extreme measures to avoid impure actions. Likewise, plucking out one's eye likely refers to extreme measures to avoid looking at others with lust.

For centuries, most people reading verse 6, followed by verses 7–9, probably assumed that this is just a co-incidence—that two different ideas were recorded consecutively, with no intrinsic connection, in the same way that ten different ideas are recorded consecutively in the Ten Commandments.

But the past twenty-plus years of crisis in the Church over the sexual abuse of children by Church ministers suggests that it may be no coincidence that these two ideas appear "overlaid" in verses 6–9. From today's perspective, it appears quite likely that the Holy Spirit intended to teach that these two ideas are actually related in Our Lord's mind. In other words, it seems as if Our Lord has intentionally conflated these two ideas by speaking about them in one breath. If so, it seems likely that He's specifically calling out, in the most severe way possible, the wrongness of sexual abuse of a child. Maybe this sin, among all others, is the greatest injustice; maybe, among all sins, this one does the most damage to individuals, to biological families, to the human family, and to the Church.

Carrie, you and other victims of sexual abuse at the hands of Church ministers have felt hopeless, as if no one shared your past and present sufferings. But these verses offer hope!

It seems likely that Our Lord had today's crisis in mind when He spoke these words two thousand years ago. This has enormous implications for both the Church and for victims. It means that this moment of crisis in the Church was already on Our Lord's mind during His ministry on earth. This crisis is shocking to us—but not to Him. From the beginning of His public ministry, He had in mind this moment of suffering, purification, and redemption for both victims and the Church.

To speak in a more personal way to you and to other victims, I propose that part of Our Lord's teaching during His earthly ministry, and part of His sufferings on Good Friday, included your sufferings and those of each individual victim of sexual abuse at the hands of Church ministers. You and other victims were *never* forgotten by Our Lord. He had your sufferings in His mind, and He endured your sufferings in a very personal way on the Cross on Good Friday. Then He redeemed them in His glorious Resurrection on Easter Sunday. This Easter redemption involves not just Him, but all victims of sexual abuse at the hands of Church ministers. Truly, this is *gospel*: "good news."

Beneath the Cross
Watercolor and pressed flowers on cold press
by Carrie Bucalo

Carrie: I painted this watercolor of Jesus on the Cross during my time as a nun in the Carmelite Monastery in Santa Fe, New Mexico. The Sangre de Cristo Mountains were breathtaking. I fell in love with the sagebrush-dotted foothills and incorporated these into several of my artworks. The lighting and colors of the New Mexican sky captivated me. Nature can be so healing!

After speaking with you, I appreciate what you've told me about your father, the memories you have of his stories told around the campfire, and the natural beauty of the Colorado mountains. You mentioned how you grieved your father after he died in 2009, and even today how the natural beauty of the mountains remains connected with your memory of your dad and his stories. Natural beauty and memory can be a powerful combination for healing.

I had the same experience in my childhood with the natural beauty of New Mexico. As a young Catholic growing up in Albuquerque, the rich heritage and faith of the people were connected in my mind with the beauty that surrounded me. I love how nature so effortlessly expresses the deeper and darker tones of human experience alongside the lightest colors and radiances. It corresponds perfectly with the life, death, and Resurrection of Our Savior.

In this painting of Good Friday, I was initially drawn by the beauty of Jesus's Mother. I was impressed with her ability to stand in the most painful place in the universe and still love God. In the Gospels, she is the one who directly encounters God, straight on. She was rooted in the Mystery, and so I painted roots shooting down from Mary, mingling with the roots from Jesus on the Cross. Mary's presence grounded me and held me fast in my deepest wound. She showed me that with eyes opened or closed, I could remain in that place, with God.

I was so moved by her invitation that I "planted" myself in this painting, represented by the flower on the back of the Cross. Through Mary's example, I wanted to be rooted in the Mystery, whether I could face God straight on or not. Surrounded by darkened foothills, Jesus hangs on the Cross, a victim Himself of injustice and hatred. This was Eden all over again, except there was a Father and Mother who refused to abandon their child, no matter what happened. Through Jesus's Resurrection, the Father proved to the world that He was bigger than Eden, and no one, not even death, could take His Child away.

Over the years, my wounds and memories have continued to heal. When I became a wife and mother, a tremendous amount of healing took place. My motherhood made my gaze stronger, and I began to recognize Christ's face in the faces of my husband and children, which is another natural wonder! Where I once felt so much pain and sorrow, I am beginning to experience healing and joy.

CHAPTER THREE

Jesus's Infinite Love for Children

"See that you do not despise one of these little ones, for I say to you that their angels in heaven always look upon the face of my heavenly Father. What is your opinion? If a man has a hundred sheep and one of them goes astray, will he not leave the ninety-nine in the hills and go in search of the stray? And if he finds it, amen, I say to you, he rejoices more over it than over the ninety-nine that did not stray. In just the same way, it is not the will of your heavenly Father that one of these little ones be lost.

(Matthew 18:10–14)

Bishop Muhm: Carrie, I'm humbled by your courage—not only in persevering in your faith, but also in sharing with me some elements of your personal journey of healing. I recognize that you've come a long way in a few years, but I'm sure that your healing continues even today and that it will continue throughout your adult life. If so, this is to be expected.

Childhood really sets the tone for the rest of our lives. What happens to each of us in childhood echoes throughout our adult life—and into eternity.

I'm afraid that perhaps one of the things you "learned" in childhood is that you didn't matter. In other words, your father's sexual desires and your mother's desire to maintain the status quo in your home life took priority over your well-being as a person and as a child of God. Of course, you were wounded very deeply by this callous disregard for your human dignity.

I hope these verses in Matthew 18 will help you on your journey of recognizing your infinite importance in the eyes of God. All children are infinitely important to Him. Thanks be to God that, through His grace, you managed to hang on to your faith life. I will hope and pray that you (and every victim of sexual abuse by those representing the Church) will take heart that Our Lord always loved you as a unique and irreplaceable child of God, infinitely valuable and important to Him. Our Lord wants to use your growing awareness of your own infinite worth and dignity to make you an instrument in healing others. The same is true for all childhood survivors of sexual abuse by those representing the Church.

Carrie: Bishop Muhm, thank you for your encouragement and for standing in the light of truth in this place. You are right—I am on a journey of healing that will continue for the rest of my life. Even though the abuse stopped nearly twenty years ago, the second- and third-order effects continue to roll downhill. For every choice made, there are both short- and long-term consequences. I lost my whole family because of the sexual abuse: mother, father, sisters, grandparents, aunts, uncles, cousins. Families are naturally designed to support and sustain every family member. But when that system is hijacked, and all the support goes toward one person—a.k.a., the abuser—then everyone else gets left behind, especially the most vulnerable members.

I'm especially sad that I have not been able to maintain relationships with my two sisters. We never had a chance to be siblings the way we wanted to. My dad worked hard to keep each of us isolated and distrustful of one another, which is very common in abusive homes. My sisters were also gravely wounded by my dad's abuses. They have many faith-wounds like my own, and because of these wounds, they seem lost to me and to the Church.

I am very encouraged by Jesus's words in Matthew 18: 10-14, that the Father does not want my sisters or me to be lost. This moves me deeply. It is very clear that Jesus will go to any length to find us. I have already been found, by Christ and by the Church, and I want my sisters to be with me, too. I want them to know the healing love of the Good Shepherd, who "laid down his life for the sheep."

In the Army we have a saying: "No soldier left behind!" As you know very well, it's been a long practice of the United States military to go back for the ones who have fallen. No one should be left behind in battle. I feel it should be the same in the Catholic Church. We are the Church Militant, and if one of our members is wounded, it should be our top priority to get them back. The lives of all childhood victims of abuse are important to God and to the Church. So is our faith.

If I may speak on behalf of victims everywhere, I can verify that yes, we were treated as objects and not as persons of infinite worth. Other people's desires came before everything else. We were made to feel small and unimportant. When we spoke, we were silenced; when we reached out for help, we were punished and isolated. But our angels really do see the face of Our Father in heaven, every moment of every day. As innocent children, we were naturally drawn to the good, the true, and the beautiful. From my experience as a survivor, there is nothing more beautiful to me than a Father who loves His children. Thankfully, Jesus shows us His Father, who is also our Father, and He stops at nothing to get His children back.

I hope and pray that every survivor will find hope in this passage of Matthew 18, and that the Church will take up Jesus's call to find the lost and invite them back. I can already imagine the healing and the rejoicing that will take place.

Bishop Muhm: Carrie, you mentioned angels because Our Lord mentioned angels in verse 10. They are very important. You might remember a series of sensational novels by Dan Brown in the decade of the 2000s. While I don't recommend them, I know they have been widely read. One of these novels was called *Angels and Demons*. That title might cause us to think more seriously about these spiritual beings.

Some people think that the tragedy of widespread sexual abuse of children by those representing the Church is the result of a demonic attack on the Church. We cannot know that, but we do know that the Church's understanding of angels and demons illustrates how important each child—and each adult—is to God.

Both Scripture and Tradition teach us that, at the dawn of creation, Our Lord created a huge number of angels. Angels are like people in some ways—but not in other ways. Like us, they have intelligence and free will. Unlike us, they don't have bodies. Because we have bodies, we learn gradually through our five senses. We can learn, grow in wisdom, change our minds, and repent. It appears likely that angels cannot do any of these things. At the moment God creates them, they already know everything they will ever know for all eternity, and once they make up their minds—either to obey God or to disobey Him—they are set on that decision for all eternity. That being said, it's quite possible that the least intelligent angel is far more intelligent than the most intelligent person in human history—and also that the weakest-willed angel has far more willpower than the strongest-willed person in human history.

As soon as God creates each angel, God allows that angel to decide freely whether to obey God's will in humility—or to rebel. Those who obey will live happily forever as God's good servants and messengers, worshipping and praising Him in heaven together with the saints.[3]

---

3 Good angels are arranged in a hierarchical structure. The Church has traditionally taught that there are nine "choirs" of good angels, ranking from highest to lowest:

1. Seraphim
2. Cherubim
3. Thrones
4. Dominions
5. Virtues

On the other hand, those angels who freely choose to rebel will live forever in misery as fallen angels, or demons, who seek to dominate other demons of lesser power and any people whom they can seduce into joining their rebellion against God. It seems that demons, like good angels, are also arranged in a hierarchical structure. Think of bullies in the schoolyard, criminal gangs on the streets of cities, or inmates in prisons . . . in each case, there's a "food chain" in which the strong dominate the weak. It's likely that the same holds true within the ranks of demons.[4]

One proof that our world is fallen—that Satan has placed his "fingerprints" on human history through original sin, which began with Satan's lies in the Garden of Eden (Genesis 3:1–20)—is that people in positions of power, including people in positions of leadership, are often tempted to dominate less powerful people. Such domination can include disrespecting, exploiting, taking advantage of, or abusing the weak.

---

6. Powers or Authorities
7. Principalities
8. Archangels
9. Angels

The Church's teaching on the hierarchy of angels is rooted in both Scripture and Church Fathers. Scriptural writings about different ranks of angels include but are not limited to: Gen. 3:24, Ex. 25:18-20, Is. 6:6, Mt. 18:10, Eph. 3:10, Col. 1:16, 1 Thess. 4:16, and Jude 1:9. Church Fathers who wrote about the nine choirs of angels include but are not limited to: St. Ignatius of Antioch, Origen, St. Athanasius, St. Gregory the Great, and St. Thomas Aquinas.

4 C.S. Lewis supports this idea in his book *The Screwtape Letters*.

Our fallen world historically has seen children as "non-persons," both because children are high maintenance, and because they do not contribute economically. Historically, "non-persons" have been subject to abuse by the powerful. (Slavery is another tragic example of this; we will consider this more fully in chapter five.)

When we combine 1) the malignant influence of demons seeking to seduce people into evil actions and sinful rebellion against God, 2) the fallen human tendency of the strong to dominate the weak, and 3) the fallen human tendency of powerful adults to consider children as "non-persons," then it's possible to understand how the tragedy of widespread sexual abuse of children can happen. When the abuser represents the Church, that makes an already tragic situation even worse.

Thanks be to God, there are many good angels, including many guardian angels. Church tradition teaches that God assigns, from among those angels who have chosen to serve Him, a guardian to watch over each person.[5] In fact, each guardian angel's primary purpose is to watch over and to help protect "their" person from evil (both physical and spiritual) during that person's short life on earth—and to worship God alongside "their" person, both in this life and in the next. Imagine! Everyone has his or her own particular guardian angel, who is probably far more intelligent and more strongly willed than the most powerful human being, and yet God assigns this angel to guard and care for them personally. This illustrates how *important* each individual human person is to God.

---

5 *Catechism of the Catholic Church*, 336.

Carrie: Bishop, I am thankful that God assigned a guardian angel to watch over me from the moment I came to be in my mother's womb. Even though I know in my head that my guardian angel was there to protect me, sometimes I still wonder why my guardian angel didn't protect me from being abused.

Bishop Muhm: Carrie, it's impossible for us to understand fully why God allows evil things to happen to good people. A full theological discussion of that perennial question would take us beyond the scope of our brief conversation here, but we can say a few things for certain:

1. God does not *cause* evil things to happen—He sometimes *allows* them to happen—for reasons we cannot see. This highlights the difference between God's *active will* and His *permissive will*.

2. God does not interfere with human free will—He allows people to choose evil freely. After all, if God didn't allow people to choose evil, then the good we choose to do would not be free either.

3. In general, if God allows evil to happen, He can and does bring good out of it. We can see many examples of this from the perspective of hindsight.

4. It's a safe bet that God does indeed stop many—or even most—potentially evil things before they happen. We cannot see most of these "preemptive" actions of God or of guardian angels.

5. In the face of the tragedy of child sexual abuse, some people might ask, "Where was God?" The only possible answer is that God was on the Cross. As I

mentioned in Chapter 2, part of the Lord's suffering on Good Friday included the suffering of each and every victim of child sexual abuse in human history.

6. When child sexual abuse happens, it's not because the child's guardian angel neglects to protect the child. In general, we see only a small part of the big picture—God alone sees the whole picture.

God does not dominate His creatures; He loves them. This love reaches its pinnacle in the crucifixion, death, and Resurrection of Jesus Christ. The humble love of Jesus Christ is countercultural in our fallen world. In verse 10, Our Lord teaches that children have guardian angels who constantly see the Father's face. Therefore, each and every child is infinitely important! Our Lord highlights this in verse 12 by His parable about the shepherd leaving the ninety-nine sheep to search for the one lost sheep. While this kind of "math" would not make sense in the cost-benefit calculus of our economically driven world, it illustrates beautifully how infinitely important *each and every* lost sheep is to Our Lord and His Heavenly Father—in childhood, in adulthood, and into eternity.

Carrie, I am sad that you and your sisters were grievously wounded and that your sisters appear to be lost. If a child victim has lost his or her faith because of sexual abuse at the hands of those who represent the Church, the Lord wants that particular individual, infinitely important child of God back *by being fully alive in the Church*. God wants your sisters back, and so do I! *No soldier left behind!* This is important and good and true and beautiful, not only for the sake of the victims themselves—but also *for the sake of the Church* and for the sake of the "ninety-nine"—an unknown (and unknowable) number of other sheep, most of whom were never abused.

The one lost sheep has an essential role to play in the sanctification and salvation of the "ninety-nine." The Father wants the "ninety-nine" to be sanctified and brought more deeply into eternal life through the holy faith life of the one who was lost but now has been found. The Father greatly desires all "one hundred" of His sheep to be fully alive. In the Lord's mysterious purposes, the one lost sheep who has allowed himself or herself to be brought back to the fold has an essential contribution to make to the "ninety-nine." The one brings many gifts that the ninety-nine wouldn't otherwise have.

As we will see in chapters four and five, such a miracle is possible. We Christians *believe in miracles*; we believe they happen *every day*; and we believe that *the Lord works His purposes through them* every day.

The Lost Sheep
Watercolor on cold press
by Carrie Bucalo

Carrie: I painted this piece when I was eighteen years old, right before I entered the Carmel of Santa Fe. I loved Matthew 18 then, just as much as I do now, although now I have come to understand its meaning more fully. The image of a shepherd leaving his ninety-nine sheep to go in search of the one lost sheep moved me deeply. In this Gospel passage, Jesus doesn't mention how the sheep got lost; He doesn't give the details. I've always imagined the lost sheep was like me. It was a little lamb, and something terrible happened to it. Maybe some of the other sheep even caused it to become lost.

As a young believer, I didn't want to leave my Catholic faith or the Good Shepherd. A tragedy happened through the actions of others in the sheepfold who tried to separate me from the fold and cast me out. I didn't want to be lost! I didn't want to be left out in the cold, dark valleys, alone and unprotected.

In many ways, I was shepherded by my guardian angel, who *always looked upon the face of my heavenly Father.* I can say with certainty that when human beings failed me, within my family and within the Catholic Church, the angelic world was there to pick up the slack. "I want to love God" was and still is the prayer of my heart. I can also say with absolute certainty that this prayer was and is enough to move heaven and earth.

There is something else very important here: From my perspective, God was my lost sheep, too. In a sense, He was lost to me by the abusive actions of my father and by other ministers in the Church. By reading the Gospels, and training my heart through prayer, I was able to hear the cry of the *Lamb of God.* I've spent my life searching for Him and allowing myself to be found by Him in the truth and beauty of my Catholic faith.

CHAPTER FOUR

A Brother Who Sins

"If your brother sins (against you), go and tell him his fault between you and him alone. If he listens to you, you have won over your brother. If he does not listen, take one or two others along with you, so that 'every fact may be established on the testimony of two or three witnesses.' If he refuses to listen to them, tell the church. If he refuses to listen even to the church, then treat him as you would a Gentile or a tax collector. Amen, I say to you, whatever you bind on earth shall be bound in heaven, and whatever you loose on earth shall be loosed in heaven. Again, (amen), I say to you, if two of you agree on earth about anything for which they are to pray, it shall be granted to them by my heavenly Father. For where two or three are gathered together in my name, there am I in the midst of them."

(Matthew 18:15–20)

Bishop Muhm: Carrie, over the past twenty years, new policies and protocols have been established in civil law and within the Church[6] to prevent children and adults from being sexually abused by those who represent the Church. Thanks be to God for that, and, please God, these new policies and protocols will succeed in eliminating sexual abuse within the Church as we move forward.

As we mentioned earlier, in this conversation you and I are not primarily focused on prevention of present or future sexual abuse of children at the hands of those who represent the Church (although, of course, that is very important). Rather, our primary focus here is to encourage the healing of abuse survivors and to do what we can to invite them to be fully alive in the Church.

In Matthew 18, Our Lord speaks with love to survivors—and to everyone else in the Church. It's obvious to everyone that human nature is fallen. People sometimes have a moral obligation to correct one another. Because nobody's perfect, any one of us might correct another person in the wrong way: either by under-correcting wrongdoing (enabling) or by overcorrecting wrongdoing (condemning). Both extremes are wrong. Part of Our Lord's plan for redemption is to introduce a template for people to correct one another in the Gospel way, which is loving and life-generating.

We might think of verses 15–20 as a blueprint for how sexual abuse of a child *ought to have been* addressed in the past when bystanders—members of the victim's family, members of the Church community, and members of society—became aware that abuse was happening. So, in this way, Our Lord is speaking to past bystanders

6 Dallas Charter of 2002; *Vos estis lux mundi* and *Affirming Our Episcopal Commitments*, both of 2019.

of sexual abuse of a child at the hands of those who represented the Church. He is also speaking to present and future bystanders who witness wrongdoing in other ways besides child sexual abuse.

But besides that, Our Lord is also speaking to present adult survivors of past child sexual abuse by those who represented the Church. You and other survivors might be challenged in trying to reconcile the Lord's teaching on how the abuse ought to have been addressed versus the reality of how it was not properly addressed—or not addressed at all—in your own experience—to your great harm.

These verses do not exempt past, present, or future bystanders from their legal or canonical responsibilities to notify proper authorities or report ongoing abuse, but they add a Gospel dimension. I hope these verses also offer adult survivors of past abuse some measure of hope based on a glimpse into the divine supernatural reconciliation between what *should have happened* and what *actually did happen.*

Carrie: Bishop Muhm, thank you for pointing out the Gospel dimension of addressing child abuse, which we find here in Matthew 18. All survivors deserve a glimpse of *what should have happened* to them. All survivors deserve to be heard and helped. I'm so thankful that Jesus did not turn a blind eye to the grave harm that some of His representatives would do to the Church and to so many innocent children. I'm also thankful that He points out how difficult it can be to correct this kind of behavior.

When I was a child, I didn't know how to protect myself or stop the abuse. Children don't know how to do those things. That's why taking advantage of a child is so unthinkably wrong. I was helpless and vulnerable in front of everyone. I really wish my parents would have listened when I told them they were hurting me. I wish my family members, who were adults, would have listened and protected my sisters and me when they saw things that were not right. I wish my teachers at school, my coaches, friends parents, pastors, and all the adults in my life would have listened and done something to help my sisters and me. I wish the police and the social workers from Child Protective Services would have helped my sisters and me when they found out about the abuse in our home. I wish the laws in our states and countries did a better job of protecting victims of childhood abuse, and their testimonies.

During my childhood, I felt utterly abandoned and betrayed by the adults in my life. I was lost to my family, my friends, my school, my community, and to the world. There seemed to be no one who would stand up to the evil of abuse on my behalf. Everyone turned a blind eye, and I felt abandoned and helpless. I really feel that they just didn't know what to do. I wished that someone, anyone, would have protected me and recognized the love I had for God.

Once again, dear Bishop, when the people who were supposed to help and protect me failed, heaven intervened.

My father began misusing the Catholic faith to manipulate and abuse me before I could read or write. He taught me how to pray the Rosary, and he told me how special Mary was. He said that he wanted me to be like Mary, because she was the "Handmaid of the Lord." Whatever God wanted, Mary agreed to do. My father twisted and misused Mary's purity to hurt me. He asked me to be "like Mary" and agree to his every wish and desire, especially if it was something sexual. My father wanted a *fiat* out of me that went against everything holy. And he didn't stop there. He took the most beautiful treasures of our faith, including the Scriptures, the Holy Eucharist, the Mass, the Seven Sacraments, and the Rosary, and he tried to weaponize them against me for his pleasures.

Bishop, I know I'm not alone. So many victims in the Church were abused like I was. There have been many priests, bishops, deacons, religious, and lay ministers of the Catholic Church, including the victim's own family members, who have misused the faith to do the most heinously evil acts to innocent children.

While my mother, along with everyone else in my community, stood by and did nothing to protect me or to stop the abuse, another Mother came to set things straight. At the very threshold of hell, it was heaven's gate that opened. I remember the day she came; it is a day I will never forget. As I played in my bedroom alone, I caught the glimmer of a mysterious light pouring in from my doorway. Only seven years old, I got up and followed the light out of my bedroom and into our family's dining room, where right in front of me stood a beautiful woman, who was brighter and more beautiful than anything I had ever seen before. Her entire body was clothed in light. She held a baby in her arms, whom I immediately recognized as the baby Jesus of Bethlehem, and a man stood behind her. I didn't know a lot about St. Joseph at the time, but thinking back on it now, it was most likely St. Joseph.

This beautiful woman looked at me and told me that what my father was telling me and what he was doing to me were very wrong. She told me that I needed to go to him and tell him that the *Mother of God* wanted him to stop touching me and my sisters immediately. He was being very disobedient. God was very angry with him. If my father stopped, God would forgive him, and my family could have Christ's light again.

Then she looked at me with so much love, and so much sadness at the same time, like she already knew what his answer was going to be, and she asked me if I would say "Yes" to God no matter what happened. When she spoke the word "Yes," I saw all the pain and the suffering that I would suffer in my life on this earth, and I began to cry because it was so much. But I also understood that she knew what this pain was like, and she would never ask me to do something she wasn't willing to do herself. I thought about it for a moment, and I continued to cry. Baby Jesus was beautiful in Mary's arms. I didn't want to say no to Him, even if it killed me, because He was helpless in front of me, and because I loved Him.

I remember looking up at Mary, feeling the weight of my whole life on my chest, and with every ounce of courage, I said "Yes" to the Mother of God, and "Yes" to the Child Jesus. I thought I was going to die right then and there. Mary smiled, and then they both disappeared.

Immediately, I went and found my father sitting on his couch, the same couch upon which he had raped and abused me on so many times already. I was afraid to speak. But seeing the Mother of God gave me the courage that I needed:

"The Mother of God wants you to stop touching me," I said.

My father sat up straight. "What did you say?" he asked, with furled eyebrows.

"What you're doing is wrong," I replied. "You're not supposed to be touching our private parts. God wants you to stop. Mary, the Mother of God, sent me to tell you."

"What!" my father yelled. His hands were clenched into tight fists. He was furious. "What do you know about the Mother of God? You are only a child. You cannot tell me what is right and what is wrong. You don't know anything!"

I ran off and hid in my closet, crying. After speaking with Mary, I knew that what my father was doing to me was wrong, and I had to do everything in my power to stay away from the abuse. But as a child, it was very difficult for me to stay away from my own parents. I sat very, very quiet in my closet for a long time. I hoped the beautiful Lady of Light would come back and tell me what to do next. But she never did, at least not in the same way.

After that day, I told my father and my mother countless times that what they were doing to me was wrong and that God and His Mother wanted the abuse to stop; I wanted the abuse to stop. But they didn't listen. They didn't listen when Child Protective Services came and told my father he needed to stop. They didn't listen when members of the Church and members of our community told him he needed to stop. They didn't listen to the laws in the State of New Mexico that stated he must stop. And they didn't listen to the courts, or to the judge.

Bishop, I'm amazed that God gave my parents so many opportunities to stop the abuse. God really does seek our conversion and wants each of us to change our stubborn hearts. Unfortunately, there are many like my parents, who refuse to listen to any kind of correction, even miraculous ones. Jesus recognized this kind of stubbornness in Matthew 18:15–17. As He describes, it requires a great amount of time and energy for everyone involved and is usually an exhausting process. But it is not impossible.

I am honestly amazed that my parents' refusal did not hinder my freedom in front of God and His proposals. Regardless of what my parents said or did, I was able to say "Yes" to God; I was able to keep my faith. I recognize now that this "Yes" belongs to each and every member of Christ's Body, the Church, because this "Yes" is part of our baptismal inheritance; it is our true treasury to which everyone has access. Survivors of abuse are no exception. God's proposals remain intact, and so does our freedom. When those who do us great harm refuse to accept correction, refuse to listen, refuse to stop, we are still free in front of God. We can prevail over every evil with the power of a "Yes."

To all survivors in the Church who were abused and told horrible lies, heaven's words are for each and every one of us: It is *not* OK for anyone to harm a child. It is *not* OK for anyone to do anything sexual to or with a child. We should be angered by these actions. Heaven is angered by these actions. God the Father is angered by these actions. The Mother of God is angered by these actions. God will judge, and the Kingdom of Heaven will prevail!

Bishop Muhm: Carrie, thank you for sharing your experiences. Your description of the abuse you suffered is so awful that it sends chills down my back. On the other hand, your encounter with Our Lady is so beautiful that it gives me goose bumps.

Our Lady told you to follow Jesus's words in Matthew 18:15: "If your brother sins (against you), go and tell him his fault between you and him alone. If he listens to you, you have won over your brother."

This important moment highlights human freedom: You were free to follow or disregard Our Lady's advice, and your father was free to continue or stop the abuse.

It has been said that most sexual abuse of children happens in the home. That is bad enough, but when the abuser represents the Church, it makes a tragic situation even worse. As you experienced, adult abusers have included Church ministers (bishops, priests, liturgical ministers, catechists, youth group leaders, etc.).

Our conversation here concerns adult victims of child sexual abuse at the hands of those representing the Church. It is likely that most of today's adult victims were abused more than twenty years ago, before canonical and legal procedures were clearly defined.

Matthew 18:15–20 suggests moral responsibility on the part of family members who discovered the abuse; like your mother, they were morally obligated to take progressive steps to stop it. When one or more family members discovered abuse in the home, they had a moral obligation to confront the abuser directly and demand that the abuse stop immediately.

- If, after that confrontation, the abuse continued, then the family member had a moral obligation to include one or two others in confronting the abuser a second time.

- If, after the second confrontation, the abuse continued, then family members had a moral obligation to include someone with authority in the Church (for example, the local parish pastor) in confronting the abuser.
- If, after that third confrontation, the abuse continued, then family members had a moral obligation to get civil authorities involved, such as police or child protective services.

I understand that your mother and other family members failed in their moral obligation to intervene; yet the moral obligation still stands.

It's important to emphasize again that our conversation here is not meant to offer legal or canonical advice. Indeed, if or when sexual abuse of a child is discovered today, the Church urges immediate recourse to canonical and legal procedures that have been established and defined within the past twenty years.

Carrie, our focus in this conversation is on the contradiction between what *should have happened* within your family years ago to stop the abuse, and what actually did not happen to stop it. This contradiction can be reconciled only in the Cross and Resurrection of Our Lord Jesus Christ. G.K. Chesterton points out that the Cross itself is a sign of contradiction.[7]

The abuse, and the suffering caused by moral failure on the part of immediate family members like your mother who became aware of it and failed to stop it, are part of the Lord's Cross as experienced by innocent

---

7 G.K. Chesterton, *The Everlasting Man*, Project Gutenberg Kindle Edition, location 2002–2044.

victims. On the other hand, your "Yes" to God and the healing the Lord achieves and greatly desires for you and other survivors are part of His Resurrection.

Jesus invites all of His disciples—and in a special way survivors of sexual abuse at the hands of those who represent the Church—to participate in His "Yes" to the Father and in Mary's "Yes" to God's promise. This communal "Yes" is part of the spiritual treasury of the Church.[8] Survivors can "spend" this spiritual treasure to keep their faith and to be fully alive in the Church.

> *"If two of you agree on earth about anything for which they are to pray, it shall be granted to them by my heavenly Father. For where two or three are gathered together in my name, there am I in the midst of them."*
>
> (Matthew 18:19-20)

---

8 The possibility of individual members of the Church benefitting from the merits of Christ and the saints is recognized in the Church's theology of indulgences. For more information on indulgences, see *Catechism of the Catholic Church*, 1471–1479.

Hope For the World
Acrylic on Canvas
by a ten-year-old abuse survivor
in the Catholic Church

Carrie: This painting was done by a young artist and abuse survivor. After going through what no child should have to endure, she took up her brush to express the hope and the wonder she still sees in the world. Planets and stars surround an earth that has been formed with continental HOPE and hearts. Two crosses, one near the top, the other near the bottom, seem to suggest a balance that can only come from Christ's presence. The light in this painting comes from the stars, reflecting the light in this young artist's heart, a heart that has suffered the worst things imaginable but still has room for the good, the true, and the beautiful.

Not long ago, I visited this young girl and her siblings. We talked about art and color, as well as our hopes and dreams for the future. These children lost their father the same way I did, but their mother is a real hero. After hearing about the abuse, she immediately corrected her husband, called the police, notified her pastor, and cooperated with the investigations. She put all her children in counseling immediately and reached out to everyone she could in the community for prayers and support.

I am amazed by this mother's strength and actions. She did the exact thing my mother should have done. It's what any parent should do the moment they find out their child has been abused. Taking the right steps not only protects children; it also prevents an abuser from doing more harm.

Bishop, I cannot even begin to tell you how beautiful that visit was. We laughed, we cried, and we felt so much hope, not only for ourselves, but for our children, for our families and for our world. Because we have a Father and Mother in heaven who love us so much, there will always be hope. If there's one thing I've learned, it's never to lose hope.

CHAPTER FIVE

The Parable of the Unforgiving Servant

Then Peter, approaching, asked him, "Lord, if my brother sins against me, how often must I forgive him? As many as seven times?" Jesus answered, "I say to you, not seven times but seventy-seven times. That is why the kingdom of heaven may be likened to a king who decided to settle accounts with his servants. When he began the accounting, a debtor was brought before him who owed him a huge amount. Since he had no way of paying it back, his master ordered him to be sold, along with his wife, his children, and all his property, in payment of the debt. At that, the servant fell down, did him homage, and said, 'Be patient with me, and I will pay you back in full.' Moved with compassion, the master of that servant let him go and forgave him the loan. When that servant had left, he found one of his fellow servants who owed him a much smaller amount. He seized him and started to choke him, demanding, 'Pay back what you owe.' Falling to his knees, his

> *fellow servant begged him, 'Be patient with me, and*
> *I will pay you back.' But he refused. Instead, he had*
> *him put in prison until he paid back the debt. Now*
> *when his fellow servants saw what had happened, they*
> *were deeply disturbed, and went to their master and*
> *reported the whole affair. His master summoned him*
> *and said to him, 'You wicked servant! I forgave you*
> *your entire debt because you begged me to. Should you*
> *not have had pity on your fellow servant, as I had pity*
> *on you?' Then in anger his master handed him over to*
> *the torturers until he should pay back the whole debt.*
> *So will my heavenly Father do to you, unless each of*
> *you forgives his brother from his heart."*
>
> (Matthew 18:21–35)

Bishop Muhm: So far in our discussion of Matthew 18, we've focused on the need for you and other adult survivors of childhood sexual abuse at the hands of those who represented the Church to be healed and to become fully alive in the Kingdom of Heaven. Each adult survivor of childhood sexual abuse is infinitely important to our Heavenly Father and is an irreplaceable citizen of the Kingdom of Heaven. Our Heavenly Father wants each adult survivor to be fully healed and fully alive in the Church, for the sake of the Church and the world.

Carrie, as part of your own healing, as part of your journey to wholeness for the sake of yourselves and others, the Lord invites you and other survivors to *forgive* both your abusers and any family members who might have enabled the abuse.

It might seem impossible for survivors to forgive abusers and those who enabled the abuse. Yet, if a survivor rules out the possibility of forgiving his or her abuser, the survivor will remain a *slave* of the abuse and will not be able to move forward in freedom; the survivor will remain trapped in the long-term slavery of mind and spirit. By definition, slaves are not free. The Lord created each one of His sheep to be truly free. Therefore, each adult survivor must follow the "underground railway" of forgiveness in order to reach the promised land of true freedom, where survivors who heal and forgive become fully alive in Christ and His Church. By the Lord's grace, forgiveness is possible; "for God all things are possible" (Matthew 19:26). That said, even after survivors forgive their abusers and enablers, the wounds of the abuse will remain. That cannot be helped. A wounded person can be free, but a slave cannot. Yet the Lord can bring new life from the wounds.

As we study and talk about Matthew 18, it's significant that the chapter ends with this parable. We must conclude that, according to Our Lord's design, part of a survivor's journey of healing and wholeness includes forgiveness.

But what does it mean to "forgive"? Forgiveness is not a denial of justice, but rather a recognition of the reality that no abuser and no enabler is presumed lost from the Lord's mercy. Forgiveness means that survivors are free to *love* their abusers and those who enabled them. Love does not mean nice feelings; it means a sincere desire—regardless of how the survivor might feel about the abuser and enablers—for those who did wrong to be made whole. Forgiveness and love are essential for survivors on the path to freedom and wholeness.

Childhood sexual abuse causes deep wounds in victims, abusers, and enablers; all need to be healed.

For a survivor to forgive and live in freedom, he or she must pray not only for their own healing but also for the healing of the abuser and enablers.

Forgiveness is *love* and *mercy*; in fact, it is Divine Mercy, which is possible only through the Lord's grace.

Carrie: Bishop, you are right. This last section of Matthew 18 is a call for forgiveness for all in this present time of the sexual abuse scandals in the Catholic Church. As a survivor in the Church, I have walked a very long path of forgiveness, and I'd like to tell you a little bit about it.

Forgiving my father who abused me, and my mother who enabled him, is like forgiving the huge debt that Jesus spoke about in Matthew 18:24. The sexual abuse of a child is a very grave offense, and there's no way abusers can ever repay their victims for what happened to them. Here Peter asks, "Lord, if my brother sins against me, how often must I forgive him? As many as seven times?" The first time I heard this parable, I was just as surprised as Peter when Jesus replied, "I say to you, not seven times but seventy-seven times."

At first, I thought—like Peter—that forgiving the ones who hurt me would be a manageable endeavor. I could just say the words, "I forgive you, Mom and Dad, for abusing me and hurting me," and that would be the end of it. But as the years have gone by, I've found that my need to forgive is more like Jesus's equation of *seventy-seven times*. Forgiveness is complex and layered, especially when a survivor is extending their heart to forgive a grave offense like abuse. Oftentimes a survivor cannot wrap their minds around the magnitude of the offense. It takes time to see it all. I've noticed that my need to forgive comes in layers and is constantly unfolding each day.

For example, when I was seven years old, I needed to forgive my father for raping and abusing me, and for twisting my faith for his pleasures. When I was fourteen, I needed to forgive him for abusing me, and for taking my friends, coaches, teachers, and schools away so he could keep me quiet about the abuse. When I was twenty-four, I needed to forgive him for having destroyed the face of family, fatherhood, and masculinity, as I sought to marry my husband and become a mother myself. I needed to forgive my father on my wedding day because he was not there to walk me down the aisle, or to dance with me for the traditional "father-daughter" dance. I needed to forgive my parents when each of my children were born for the traumatic scars that remained in me, which made childbirth very painful. And now my husband, children, and I need to forgive them every day, when we feel the absence of parents and grandparents in our lives.[9]

As the days and years have gone by, the need to forgive my parents throughout my day has steadily increased. I would have never imagined that it would take so much effort and perseverance on my part, but I am comforted that Jesus knew about this and proposed it here in Matthew 18.

I am finding that grave offenses like child sexual abuse do not stay in the past like everyone would like. These wounds are very active in the present and the future because of the magnitude and the weight that

---

9 The imagery of forgiving someone over time was introduced in another story by Genevieve Kineke, talk on forgiveness, Pilgrim Center of Hope Catholic Women's Conference, July 17, 2021.

was attached to them. It was my very being, the depths of my heart and soul, that were harmed.

This has been made very clear by the experiences of those closest to me who are also affected by these wounds. For example, Justin has had to be more patient and more self-effacing than any man I know because of what happened to me. He has gone with me to many therapy sessions to help me navigate through my PTSD, trauma responses, dissociation, etc. And every time I've had to stop and process a memory, or a trauma response, he's had to face what my father did to me and forgive him.

My children are also affected by these wounds. Every time I stop and process a memory and work through my trauma responses, it takes time away from them and our family. Thank God these "tactical pauses" are requiring less and less physical time for me as the years go by. But this is a loss that my children experience, a direct result from my childhood of abuse. As my children grow up and begin to process these losses, and other losses like the missing grandparents and extended family in their lives, they will also be called to forgive.

Not too long ago, one of my daughters confided to me that she secretly hopes her class at school will never do a family tree project because she is overwhelmed with anxiety thinking about what she'd do with the lines for the names of my mother and father. She didn't want to tell her class that her grandpa lives in prison, or even worse, that he's a child abuser. My heart broke when she told me this, but it's true. This is a devastating wound that my children must face. I'm sure there will be many things like this in their lives that they will need to process and forgive. I'm sure my parents never imagined the scope of their offense or calculated how it would affect future generations, but it did. Wounds like these cut deep.

As you can see, forgiving offenses like this is a TALL order, as it requires the heart to say: "I forgive," sometimes seventy-seven times in one day. It is not something that can be done all at once, but it takes time and a lot of perseverance.

For someone to forgive a grave offense, they need to be given the proper amount of time and help to process, grieve, and understand what they are forgiving. They must come to terms with the reality of what happened to them, so they can forgive the actual offense and not some watered-down version of it.

The king in Jesus's parable was able to forgive the huge debt because he knew the magnitude of it, and he was willing to accept the loss for the sake of his servant's life. Forgiveness does not mean that one's personal treasury will be restored, only one's heart. Forgiving these kinds of *debts* may make survivors feel raw, vulnerable, and overwhelmed. It takes time, and may require a lot of help from counselors, therapists, and trusted friends. But it is possible!

The way family and friends can help survivors to forgive is by remembering that the survivor is the primary victim. Secondary or more removed persons may be able to forgive their piece easily. But a survivor's need to forgive will most likely be complex and layered and will need to be taken moment by moment, day by day. If survivors are truly expected to forgive *seventy-seven times . . . from the heart*, as Jesus proposes, then it would be a great act of charity on everyone's behalf to protect their acts of forgiveness, and not rush or diminish the process.[10]

For survivors, "forgive and forget" is not possible. We will always remember. As Catholic speaker Genevieve Kineke said at a women's conference I attended in 2021, "Amnesia is in the manual of disorders—as you forgive, the memories are transformed."[11] With God's help, our memories can open up to His presence on the Cross, and the healing of His Resurrection. I have found great encouragement and hope in God's transforming memories.[12]

A huge hurdle that survivors need to overcome is the general misunderstanding that forgiveness takes away the pain. I personally struggled with this for years. I thought that the truer my heart was, and the more I forgave, the less I'd suffer. Sadly, this has not been the case. Even though I've been working through the forgiveness process my entire life, my wounds have remained, and they hurt me deeply, every single day. This pain has pushed me and made me question the authenticity of my forgiveness. But over the years, I've come to see it in a different light.

Forgiving a large debt does not mean that what was lost is somehow instantly restored. It means that the

---

10 These concepts of helping someone to forgive were introduced by Genevieve Kineke, talk on forgiveness, Pilgrim Center of Hope Catholic Women's Conference, July 17, 2021.

11 Genevieve Kineke, talk on forgiveness, Pilgrim Center of Hope Catholic Women's Conference, July 17, 2021.

12 See "Memories of God" in Carrie Bucalo's essay *The Spiritual Journey of Healing*.

one who forgives is willing to live with the loss, even if it is a great one. As survivors in the Church forgive their abusers and those who enabled them, they must know that forgiveness will not take away their pain, the memories, or the losses in their life. However, forgiveness will make them able to love greatly, in all the ways they wished they could have been loved by others.

In my "yes" to God, there was also my agreement to forgive my father for abusing and traumatizing me, to forgive my mother for enabling him to do so, to forgive my extended family members who could have helped me but did nothing to stop the abuse, to forgive my community for turning a blind eye to the abuse, to forgive the local lawmakers and authorities who did not protect me, and to forgive the leadership in the Catholic Church for what some have done . . . and for what some have failed to do.

I am happy to tell you, dear Bishop, that I have chosen to live with these losses, because I want to love greatly. I want to love my husband and children with all my heart. I want to love my community with all my heart. I want to love my country with all my heart. I want to love my Church with all my heart. I want to love the world with all my heart. And I want to love God with all my heart. And the only way to do that is by reclaiming all the pieces.

Bishop Muhm: Carrie, as we have discussed, Our Lord's insistence on forgiveness is very challenging for survivors. If a survivor (through God's grace) has been able to move beyond hatred of their abuser and enablers, they might feel that the best they can do is to forget about the abuse. But as you say, forgetting will not be possible; survivors will have to make conscious choices to forgive. Our Lord insists that people must make a conscious choice to forgive those who have wronged them. He illustrates it in a vivid way through this parable.

Again, forgiveness does not mean that we *deny* the abuse happened, nor that we *forget* about the abuse, nor that we pretend the abuse wasn't important. Forgiveness does not mean that we manufacture nice feelings of affection toward the abuser and those who enabled, nor does it mean that the survivor must advocate for dismissal of legal charges or penalties against the abuser. No . . . forgiveness means none of these things.

Forgiveness is not a denial of reality; it is not a denial of justice; it is not rooted in *feelings*; rather, forgiveness is *a decision* that the survivor makes to live free of the abuse, being set free of slavery and moving forward in freedom. The Lord comes to set captives free (see Luke 4:18, 21).

Forgiveness begins when the survivor realistically acknowledges that the abuser and enablers—like the survivor, and like every other human person—are made in the image and likeness of God. Everyone is made in the image and likeness of God, so everyone is worthy of love. Our Lord tells us to love our enemies (Matthew 5:44). As we noted earlier, love means willing the good of another. But part of love is to hold people accountable for their actions. This accountability is for the moral development of the wrongdoer and for the protection of society, so that the abuser will be less likely to abuse others in the future.

Love demands justice. Cardinal John O'Connor was Archbishop of New York from 1984–2000. He ordained me to the priesthood. His episcopal motto was "There can be no love without justice."

In December 1983, Pope Saint John Paul II went to a Rome prison to visit Ali Agca, the man who had shot him in 1981. After the visit, a reporter asked the pope if he had forgiven and prayed for Agca. The pope replied, "Certainly." Then the reporter asked if the Pope would advocate for Agca's early release from prison. The pope replied, "Certainly not." It is possible—and necessary—to ensure that abusers are held legally accountable while at the same time striving to love and forgive them.

Love demands justice. Love also requires a survivor to pray for the abuser, that the abuser will grow up psychologically and spiritually.

Carrie, as you said, sexual abuse of children by those who represent the Church causes complex problems for survivors all through adulthood. It also reveals complex problems that already existed within abusers and enablers.

In the moral arena, those who commit sexual abuse of a child, or those who enabled the abuse, certainly have committed mortal sins. They can be forgiven and healed through the sacraments of healing and purification (Baptism, Reconciliation, and Anointing of the Sick). Our faith teaches us that no sin is so bad that it cannot be forgiven through the death and Resurrection of Our Lord Jesus Christ. The Lord's mercy, called *Divine Mercy*, is always bigger than our sins—and bigger even than our capacity to sin.

In the psychological arena, sexual abuse of a child or the enabling of such abuse reveals deep wounds or immaturity on the part of the abuser or enabler. These wounds or immaturity can and should be addressed though clinical therapy on the psychological level, with trust in God's supernatural grace. Part of a survivor's journey of healing is to pray for the abuser and enablers to be made whole.

How can the horrific suffering caused by the abuse be reconciled with love—the survivor willing good for their abuser and enablers? This reconciliation can happen only in the Cross and Resurrection of Jesus Christ. On the Cross, Jesus reconciles justice, love, forgiveness, and mercy. In His Resurrection, the wounds that killed Him become a source of new life.

After Our Lord resurrected on Easter Sunday, He still bore the wounds of His crucifixion. He showed these wounds to the Apostle Thomas on the evening of Easter Sunday (see John 20:27–28) and invited Thomas to touch the wounds. When Thomas touched them, he was healed of his previous unbelief. After the Resurrection, Our Lord's wounds no longer hurt Him nor drained Him of life; after the Resurrection, the wounds were glorious, healing and generating new life in those who touched them.

A survivor who is able (through God's grace) to forgive and love the abuser and enablers has access to new life in abundance; the survivor is now living on earth the new and eternal life of the Risen Christ. Forgiveness means that although the wounds of the abuse remain in the survivor (and will remain eternally), the wounds have become *redeemed*, in the pattern of Our Lord's redeemed wounds on Easter Sunday night. Now, the redeemed wounds are glorious—they generate new life in the survivor—and through him or her, they generate new life in others. The wounds give the survivor a great capacity to evangelize others and draw them to eternal life in the crucified and risen Savior.

Our Lord carries His redeemed wounds with Him into eternity. So will His disciples who are survivors of child sexual abuse. But now their wounds will generate life—not drain it.

In the 1700s, John Cennick and Charles Wesley wrote a wonderful Christian Advent hymn titled "Lo, He Comes." This beautiful classic hymn tells the story of the Second Coming of Christ. The words highlight that at His Second Coming, the Risen Christ continues to bear the wounds he suffered on Good Friday—and He will continue to bear them forever. But now the wounds are *glorious:*

> *Those dear tokens of His passion*
> *Still His dazzling body bears,*
> *Cause of endless exultation*
> *To His ransomed worshippers;*
> *With what rapture, with what rapture,*
> *Gaze we on those glorious scars.*

Carrie, I hope you and other survivors of childhood sexual abuse at the hands of those who represented the Church will be confident that your wounds, which you will carry with you into eternity, are destined to be redeemed and glorified by the grace of the Risen Christ. The Lord invites you to unite your wounds with His glorified wounds, so that your wounds will generate new life in yourself and in others.

All of us—survivors, abusers, and enablers; innocent bystanders; laypeople and clergy; men and women; adults and children—must finally put our hope and confidence in the Risen Christ. As a bishop, my own episcopal motto is "He Is Risen." The Resurrection of Christ guarantees that ultimately:

- Freedom will triumph over slavery.
- Good will triumph over evil.
- Truth will triumph over lies.
- Love will triumph over hatred.
- Justice will triumph over injustice.
- Mercy will triumph over vindictiveness.
- Life will triumph over death.

Fruitful
Watercolor on cold press
by Carrie Bucalo

Carrie: As a survivor, I've had so many uncertainties and doubts about my love for God, and about the darkness and seemingly endless weight of the crosses in my life. Honestly, I've been tempted to despair on many occasions because of these factors. The one thing that has kept me going are the amazing fruits this struggle has born. This painting reflects the fruits of the heart that are very difficult to measure: faith, hope, love, forgiveness, and mercy.

Fruitfulness of spirit is not about how large or how strong the heart is. It's all about the flavor, dynamism, and richness of the heart. The fruits of the spirit are *love, joy, peace, patience, kindness, goodness, generosity, gentleness, faithfulness, modesty, self-control, and chastity.* Our Lord once said, "You shall know a tree by its fruits" (Matthew 7:20). I like to think that each one of us has a knowable heart, like His, made to produce rich fruits that others can see and taste for themselves.

In this painting, I show how freedom has triumphed over slavery, good has conquered evil, truth has prevailed over the lies, love has overcome hatred, justice has triumphed over injustice, mercy reigns over vindictiveness, and life has conquered death. The Cross is always there, with its crown of thorns, but as you said so beautifully, Bishop, *God's mercy and love are bigger than our capacity to sin.*

These fruits have given me the courage to consider that God's love *is* bigger than what happened to me. This is miraculous. Something and Someone is bigger than the darkness, pain, and damage left behind by the abuse. There is a way through; our story does not end in defeat.

CONCLUSION

Where Do We Go from Here?

Bishop Muhm: Carrie, you and I have had a very important conversation. You represent survivors of sexual abuse at the hands of those who represent the Church, and I represent the Church. For me, our conversation has been a big step in understanding some of the complexity and far-reaching consequences of such abuse, which has been openly acknowledged in the Church for only about twenty years.

In 1 Corinthians 12:26, St. Paul says, "If [one] part (of the body) suffers, all the parts suffer with it; if one part is honored, all the parts share its joy." It's safe to say that many members of the Church who suffered childhood sexual abuse at the hands of someone who represented the Church seem to be lost to the Church—people like your sisters, whom you mentioned in Chapter 3. Their absence from the Church is a grave loss for the entire Church community. The Lord wants each of these lost sheep back.

On the other hand, when one survivor remains in the Church or returns to the Church—someone like you—with their faith strengthened, then that survivor is an incalculable gift to the entire Church community. New life in abundance will flow through that renewed survivor to benefit all.

In this conversation, you and I have tried to explore some of what Matthew 18 teaches adult survivors of sexual abuse at the hands of someone who represented the Church. We hope that these survivors might be able, with God's grace, to move forward toward becoming fully alive in Christ. We haven't considered everything that could be learned in Matthew 18, but I for one have learned a great deal from our conversation. I hope that at least one survivor has learned something that might be helpful to them in their journey to become fully alive in Christ.

Although I was never sexually abused by anyone, our conversation has challenged me to open myself in new ways to allow the Lord's grace to heal and redeem my own brokenness and woundedness. I hope our conversation will facilitate healing and conversion in at least one survivor, not only for their own sake as a survivor, but also for the sake of those whom the Lord intends to evangelize through them. If at least one reader will grow and heal as a person from our conversation, we can be sure that the Lord will use them to evangelize others. When that happens, then the Lord, who brings new life out of death, will generate new learning and new life in each person who reaches out in Christian charity to others.

As I say, I hope we've contributed to renewal and conversion in at least one person. If so, then we have contributed to the renewal of the Church and the world. In His glorious Resurrection from the dead, the Lord brings something out of nothing. There's no limit to the good that the Lord can bring about in the lives of many people, through one survivor becoming more fully alive in Christ. Please God, that miraculous reality will become a reality in my life and in yours, Carrie, as well as in the lives of our readers.

Carrie: Bishop, thank you for talking with me, and for being present in this painful, yet redeeming place. This conversation with you has been truly healing. I trust the healing will continue far into the future. I am one person this conversation has already helped, and I believe there will be many others.

With the Gospel message as our guide, you and I have looked at the sexual abuse scandal in the Catholic Church straight on and we have seen that Christ is here, and He is risen! Thank you, Bishop, for believing with me. Thank you for hoping with me. Thank you for being present to the love that so many people have for God and neighbor in this place.

While history will forever point to the day the scandals in the Catholic Church began, Christ will always point to the day the scandals ended. And it may very well look like this: the day when all the members of Christ's Body, the Church, are accounted for; the day *the little ones who believe in Him* are heard, found, and loved.

I think we may be peering at the other side of this scandal, dear Bishop! Perhaps it's only the mustard seed view of it, but I believe it's happening right now. Many survivors, like me, are slowly but surely being healed by Truth, and I hope this conversation gives everyone a reason and a chance to believe again.

Forward, dear Bishop! Forward! The way to the future Church is forward![13] I believe we can be a people who say "Yes" to God, no matter what happens.

---

13 See homily of Pope Francis at the September 2015 Canonization Mass of St. Junipero Serra. The Holy Father ends his homily as follows: "Father Serra had a motto which inspired his life and work, not just a saying, but above all a reality which shaped the way he lived: *siempre adelante!* Keep moving forward! For him, this was the way to continue experiencing the joy of the Gospel, to keep his heart from growing numb, from being anesthetized. He kept moving forward, because the Lord was waiting. He kept going, because his brothers and sisters were waiting. He kept going forward to the end of his life. Today, like him, may we be able to say: Forward! Let's keep moving forward!"

Risen
Mixed Media
by Carrie, Angelina, and Elijah Bucalo

The Monarch Butterfly
by Carrie Bucalo

You perch before me,
a message on golden wing,
announcing my *unexpected salvation*.

Is this how heaven comes to earth?
Like black-framed stained glass,
fluttering beside me.

Your presence pollinates
my mind with memories
of people and places long ago.

A sweetness I had lost
comes back to me now,
as you dance on a flower.

You are linked
with God's own mind…
perhaps you are his clearest thought.

Starting out as *a worm,*
and not a man,
where did you find such wisdom?

What convinced you to halt your
crawling on this lowly earth?
I've hardly met a man who would do the same.

You found your branch and anchored deep.
Outstretched, you hung
like God himself.

My heart often stops
with the pain of death,
and the question of the tomb.

But you heard heaven and the open sky
in his words:
'Take up your cross and follow me.'

Perhaps I should join you,
encased in this moment.
Will I become something entirely new?

A miracle no one can explain:
Kings and Queens fly with angels,
Maranatha.

About the Authors

Carrie Bucalo is an Army wife, mother, watercolor artist, and writer. She was born and raised in Albuquerque, New Mexico. After being sexually abused for eighteen years by her biological father, an active lay minister in the Catholic Church, she ran away from home and joined the Carmelite Monastery of Santa Fe. There she studied the ancient ways of Carmelite prayer and mysticism. For three years she lived in silence and solitude and learned to navigate through the "Dark Night of the Soul," ultimately finding a way to communicate her faith-wounds to others. Her father was arrested for child sexual abuse in 2002, and Carrie became involved in an unbearable court battle that has spanned over two decades and is still ongoing.

In 2005, Carrie married Justin Bucalo, a youth minister at a large church in Rio Rancho, New Mexico. Justin joined the United States Army in 2010, and the couple loves moving around the world with their children, as they serve their country.

In 2010, Carrie founded the website, www. healedbytruth.com, to share her essays, *The Spiritual Journey of Healing*, and to promote faith-healing for abuse survivors and their families. For the past two decades, Carrie has advocated for the spiritual needs of abuse survivors in the Catholic Church, and she writes for the bestselling *Magnificat*.

Bishop Bill Muhm was raised in Denver, Colorado. He earned a BS in Business Administration from Colorado State University in 1980. He served on active duty in the Navy as a Supply Corps officer, as a civilian accountant, and as part owner of a family pizza business before entering the minor seminary in 1989 to study for the Catholic priesthood. He was ordained a priest for the Archdiocese of New York in 1995 by John Cardinal O'Connor. After serving at civilian parishes in Ossining, NY, and Staten Island, NY, he returned to active duty as a Navy chaplain in 1998. His military assignments included shipboard and shore-based duty in Japan, Iraq, and the USA. Bishop Muhm retired from the Navy in 2018, with the rank of Navy Captain. In 2019, he was ordained an Auxiliary Bishop and Vicar for Europe and Asia for the Archdiocese for the Military Services, USA. He currently lives in Germany and shepherds the U.S. Catholic communities at military installations in Europe, Asia, and Guam.

www.ingramcontent.com/pod-product-compliance
Lightning Source LLC
Chambersburg PA
CBHW051642120626
46551CB00015B/2189